MULTIPLE SKILLS SERIES: Reading

Third Edition

Richard A. Boning

SRA McGraw-Hill

Columbus, Ohio

A Division of The McGraw-Hill Companies

Cover, Doug Armand/Tony Stone Images

SRA/McGraw-Hill
A Division of The **McGraw·Hill** *Companies*

Copyright © 1998 by SRA/McGraw-Hill. All rights reserved.
Except as permitted under the United States Copyright Act, no
part of this publication may be reproduced or distributed in any
form or by any means, or stored in a database or retrieval
system, without prior written permission from the publisher.

Printed in the United States of America.

Send all inquiries to:
SRA/McGraw-Hill
250 Old Wilson Bridge Road
Suite 310
Worthington, Ohio 43085

ISBN 0-02-688417-8

4 5 6 7 8 9 SCG 02 01 00 99

To the Teacher

PURPOSE
The *Multiple Skills Series* is a nonconsumable reading program designed to develop a cluster of key reading skills and to integrate these skills with each other and with the other language arts. *Multiple Skills* is also diagnostic, making it possible for you to identify specific types of reading skills that might be causing difficulty for individual students.

FOR WHOM
The twelve levels of the *Multiple Skills Series* are geared to students who comprehend on the pre-first- through ninth-grade reading levels.
- The Picture Level is for children who have not acquired a basic sight vocabulary.
- The Preparatory 1 Level is for children who have developed a limited basic sight vocabulary.
- The Preparatory 2 Level is for children who have a basic sight vocabulary but are not yet reading on the first-grade level.
- Books A through I are appropriate for students who can read on grade levels one through nine respectively. Because of their high interest level, the books may also be used effectively with students functioning at these levels of competence in other grades.

The **Multiple Skills Series Placement Tests** will help you determine the appropriate level for each student.

PLACEMENT TESTS
The Elementary Placement Test (for grades Pre-1 through 3) and the Midway Placement Tests (for grades 4–9) will help you place each student properly. The tests consist of representative units selected from the series. The test books contain two forms, X and Y. One form may be used for placement and the second as a posttest to measure progress. The tests are easy to administer and score. Blackline Masters are provided for worksheets and student performance profiles.

THE BOOKS
This third edition of the *Multiple Skills Series* maintains the quality and focus that have distinguished this program for over 25 years. The series includes four books at each level, Picture Level through Level I. Each book in the Picture Level through Level B contains 25 units. Each book in Level C through Level I contains 50 units. The units within each book increase in difficulty. The books within a level also increase in difficulty—Level A, Book 2 is slightly more difficult than Level A, Book 1, and so on. This gradual increase in difficulty permits students to advance from one book to the next and from one level to the next without frustration.

To the Teacher

Each book contains an **About This Book** page, which explains the skills to the students and shows them how to approach reading the selections and questions. In the lowest levels, you should read About This Book to the children.

The questions that follow each unit are designed to develop specific reading skills. In the lowest levels, you should read the questions to the children.

In Levels A and B, the question pattern in each unit is
1. Title (main idea)
2. Stated detail
3. Stated detail
4. Inference or conclusion
5. Picture clue

The **Language Activity Pages** (LAP) in each level consist of four parts: Exercising Your Skill, Expanding Your Skill, Exploring Language, and Expressing Yourself. These pages lead the students beyond the book through a broadening spiral of writing, speaking, and other individual and group language activities that apply, extend, and integrate the skills being developed. You may use all, some, or none of the activities in any LAP; however, some LAP activities depend on preceding ones. In the lowest levels, you should read the LAPs to the children.

In Level B, each set of Language Activity Pages focuses on a particular skill developed through the book:

First LAP	Details
Second LAP	Picture interpretations
Third LAP	Main ideas
Last LAP	Inferences and conclusions

SESSIONS

The *Multiple Skills Series* is an individualized reading program that may be used with small groups or an entire class. Short sessions are the most effective. Use a short session every day or every other day, completing a few units in each session. Time allocated to the Language Activity Pages depends on the abilities of the individual students.

SCORING

Students should record their answers on the reproducible worksheets. The worksheets make scoring easier and provide uniform records of the children's work. Using worksheets also avoids consuming the books.

Because it is important for the students to know how they are progressing, you should score the units as soon as they've been completed. Then you can discuss the questions and activities with the students and encourage them to justify their responses. Many of the LAPs are open-ended and do not lend themselves to an objective score; for this reason, there are no answer keys for these pages.

About This Book

When you read a story, you read words and sentences that belong together. They all help to tell about one **main idea**. Read this story. Think about what it is mainly about.

> Ann had a green plant. It began to look brown. She gave her plant water. She put it in the sun. Soon the plant was green again.

Do all of the sentences in the story tell about Ann's plant? Would "Ann's Plant" be a good title for the story? Figuring out what a story is mainly about is an important reading skill.

Another important reading skill is remembering the facts, or **details**, in a story. In the story above, what was the girl's name? What was wrong with her plant? A good reader pays attention to the facts.

A good reader also figures out **things that the writer does not say**. What did Ann do for her plant? Why do you think she did these things? The story does not tell you that green plants need water and sunlight, but you can figure this out from what the story tells you. Good readers think about what the story tells them. They figure things out as they read.

Sometimes a story has a **picture** to go with it. The picture may tell you things that the words do not. The picture can help tell the story.

In this book, there are twenty-five stories. Read each story and look at the picture that goes with it. Then choose a good **title**, or name, for the story. Answer the questions about what the story and the picture tell you.

UNIT 1

Each summer, a child from the city goes to stay with the Cruz family for a few weeks. The Cruz family lives in the country near a lake. There is space to play and clean air.

This summer, Ana went for a visit. Going to the country was a special treat for Ana. Two of the Cruz children, Carmen and Rey, were about the same age as Ana. Ana wanted to do things that she couldn't do in the city. The children went swimming in the lake. They put up a tent in the backyard and slept there. They went fishing. They went hiking in the woods. Ana learned to ride a bike. Everyone had a good time.

UNIT 1

1. The best title is—

    (A) At the Lake

    (B) A Trip to the City

    (C) Ana Visits in the Country

    (D) Ana Camps Out

2. Ana learned to—

    (A) fix a tent (B) swim

    (C) ride a bike (D) read

3. The children—

    (A) went to a circus (B) slept in a tent

    (C) had a party (D) went to the city

4. You can tell that Ana—

    (A) was cold (B) liked the country

    (C) wanted to go home (D) went by train

5. In the picture, the children are—

    (A) in the woods (B) on a boat

    (C) in the water (D) in the house

UNIT 2

Linda and Barry were exploring. They found a cave and walked a little way inside. It was dark, so Linda went to her house to get a flashlight. When she came back, the opening of the cave was gone! Some rocks had fallen and covered the opening. Barry was caught inside.

Linda began moving the rocks. She used a big stick to move a very big rock. Finally, she reached Barry. He was all right.

Linda and Barry still explore together, but they stay away from caves.

UNIT 2

1. The best title is—
   - (A) Fun at the Park
   - (B) Linda Finds a Flashlight
   - (C) Linda Saves Barry's Life
   - (D) Barry Runs Away

2. Linda and Barry were exploring a—
   - (A) house
   - (B) cave
   - (C) car
   - (D) lake

3. Linda pushed away a big rock with—
   - (A) a bat
   - (B) her hands
   - (C) a stick
   - (D) her feet

4. When Barry was caught in the cave, he was probably—
   - (A) afraid
   - (B) happy
   - (C) singing
   - (D) reading

5. In the picture, the children are—
   - (A) resting
   - (B) fishing
   - (C) sleeping
   - (D) looking

UNIT 3

Mr. Young lived by a lake. He wanted to move his house to the other side. It was winter and there was ice on the lake. Mr. Young thought, "I'll put my house on a big truck. Then I can drive it across the ice to the other side."

The house was put on a big truck, and Mr. Young began driving the truck across the lake. When he was in the middle, he heard a crack. Then the ice broke! The truck and Mr. Young's house sank to the bottom. Mr. Young was saved, but he had lost his house.

UNIT 3

1. The best title is—

   (A) Mr. Young Loses His House

   (B) Swimming at the Lake

   (C) A Nice Drive

   (D) Mr. Young Buys a House

2. Mr. Young put his house on a—

   (A) car   (B) train

   (C) truck   (D) plane

3. Mr. Young moved his house in the—

   (A) summer   (B) winter

   (C) spring   (D) fall

4. The water in the lake must have been—

   (A) hot   (B) dry

   (C) red   (D) cold

5. In the picture, the house on the truck has—

   (A) people inside   (B) a garage

   (C) two windows   (D) three doors

UNIT 4

On Saturday, Sandy rides her pet to the store. People laugh in a friendly way and wave at her. They laugh because Sandy's pet is a pig! Sandy was given the pig when it was only a baby. But soon it weighed over two hundred pounds. Sandy calls it Snowy.

Every Saturday, Sandy rides Snowy into town. She goes to the store and buys a treat for the pig. She finds something different every week. After she leaves the store, Sandy climbs on her pet and rides home.

UNIT 4

1. The best title is—

    (A) Sandy Rides in a Race

    (B) Living on a Farm

    (C) Sandy and Her Pet Pig

    (D) How to Ride a Horse

2. Sandy goes to the store to buy—

    (A) a treat　　　　　(B) toys

    (C) peanuts　　　　(D) a paper

3. When the people see Sandy and Snowy, they—

    (A) cry　　　　　　(B) laugh

    (C) run away　　　 (D) pet the pig

4. Sandy calls her pig Snowy because it is—

    (A) smart　　　　　(B) white

    (C) big　　　　　　(D) small

5. In the picture, the girl is—

    (A) reading in school　　(B) painting a wagon

    (C) on a lake　　　　　　(D) in a store

UNIT 5

Grandpa, Sam, and Kate sat on the porch. Grandpa said, "It feels and looks like spring."

"What do you mean, Grandpa?" asked Sam.

"Well," said Grandpa, "come for a walk with me and keep your eyes open."

Grandpa pointed to a tree branch. Kate and Sam saw a bud. "Soon that will turn into a leaf. New green leaves on a tree mean spring."

Kate saw something. She said, "Mother's flowers are coming up. That happens when it is spring."

Sam added, "It feels warmer outside, and I can play outside longer."

UNIT 5

1. The best title is—

    (A) Grandpa
    (B) Growing Flowers
    (C) Spring Is Here
    (D) Spring Is Over

2. The story says that when spring comes—

    (A) there is snow
    (B) days get colder
    (C) leaves fall off
    (D) flowers come up

3. Grandpa asked Kate and Sam to—

    (A) go for a walk
    (B) come to dinner
    (C) listen to a story
    (D) come inside

4. You can tell this story takes place—

    (A) inside
    (B) at night
    (C) outside
    (D) in the cold

5. In the picture, Kate has found—

    (A) a leaf
    (B) a bird
    (C) money
    (D) a flower coming up

UNIT 6

Most pet shows are for good-looking animals. Prizes are given for the most beautiful dog and cat. A different kind of pet show was held not long ago. It was a show for ugly animals!

Mrs. Clover had a dog named Pug. She loved Pug very much. She never put him in a pet show—because Pug was so ugly. Mrs. Clover thought, "I'll have a pet show for ugly animals."

People brought a hundred pets to the show. There were many ugly dogs and cats, but Pug won first prize.

UNIT 6

1. The best title is—

    (A) A Beautiful Cat Wins First Prize

    (B) Mrs. Clover Finds Her Dog

    (C) A Pet Show for Ugly Animals

    (D) Teaching Animals Tricks

2. Pug was—

    (A) a cute cat (B) an ugly dog
    (C) a small rabbit (D) an unhappy duck

3. Most pet shows are for—

    (A) good-looking animals (B) snakes and turtles
    (C) ugly elephants (D) small birds

4. You can tell that there are *not* many pet shows for—

    (A) dogs (B) cats
    (C) ugly animals (D) good-looking animals

5. In the picture, there are—

    (A) three cats (B) two cats
    (C) two dogs (D) four dogs

The First L A P
Language Activity Pages

A. Exercising Your Skill

A year has four parts called seasons. The four seasons are winter, spring, summer, and fall. The stories in Units 1, 3, and 5 tell about things that happened in summer, winter, and spring. Read each story again and look at the pictures. Also, think about what happens in the fall. Which season is your favorite one? On your own paper, make a word map like the one started below. But make your word map for the season you like best. In the middle circle write a word that tells the season. Then write words in the other circles that tell about your favorite season.

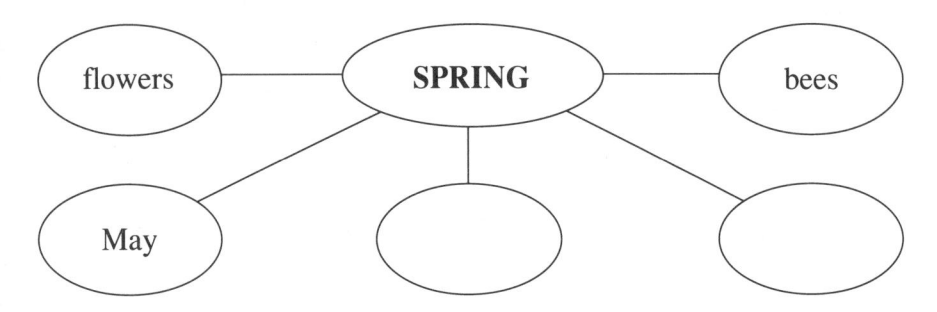

flowers — SPRING — bees

May

Share your word map with your class. Tell why you like your favorite season.

B. Expanding Your Skill

Below are some silly sentences about the seasons. One part of each sentence is wrong. Change the words that are not right. Write the new words on your paper.

1. In summer, the sky is green where we live.
2. Some people bring snow suits to the pond in the summer.
3. My friend and I plant red and yellow leaves in the fall.
4. In spring new buds open and the leaves turn blue.

The First L A P
Language Activity Pages

C. Exploring Language

Read this story about the four seasons. On your paper, write one thing about each season.

> We live on the earth. The earth moves around the sun. Each "trip" takes 365 days, or one year. When the place on the earth where you live is near the sun, it is summer. In summer, the days are long and very warm. When the place where you live is away from the sun, it is winter. In winter, the days are shorter and colder.
>
> When spring comes, the earth gets warmer. Flower buds begin to open. In the summer, crops and plants grow. In the fall, leaves fall off the trees. Birds and animals get ready for winter. Birds may fly to warmer places, and animals grow coats of fur. In winter, the trees have no leaves. Then they seem to be not living. But they are only resting. Some animals, such as the bear and frog, sleep all winter.

1. Summer _____
2. Fall _____
3. Winter _____
4. Spring _____

If you can, add one thing about what the seasons are like where you live.

D. Expressing Yourself

Do one of these things.

1. Write a story about the time of year you like best. Tell what you do, what the earth looks like, and if it is hot or cold, warm or cool.

2. Draw a picture of each time of year. Write sentences about each picture.

UNIT 7

Sam Brooks was a mail carrier. He walked 13 miles every day for 21 years. When Sam stopped working, he said, "I've walked enough. Now I'm going to ride."

Since then, Sam has been riding. He rides buses all around the country. He has ridden over 100,000 miles and visited every state. Sam likes riding in buses because he can talk to many different people. He also likes it because he isn't walking.

Sam may start taking some train rides next. Maybe you will meet him one day!

UNIT 7

1. The best title is—

   (A) A Trip Across the Country

   (B) A Mail Carrier Who Likes to Walk

   (C) A Man Who Likes to Ride on Buses

   (D) Sam Brooks Writes a Letter

2. The story says that Sam has visited every—

   (A) city   (B) school

   (C) state   (D) farm

3. Now Sam wants to—

   (A) fly an airplane   (B) ride trains

   (C) become a teacher (D) be in a circus

4. You can tell that Sam now spends a lot of time—

   (A) singing   (B) eating

   (C) running   (D) sitting

5. In the picture, two men are wearing—

   (A) ties   (B) hats

   (C) gloves   (D) glasses

UNIT 8

Maria went to the library. She wanted to write a report for school. She wanted to tell about things we have today that people didn't have long ago. She also wanted to tell about things that people today are trying to make. This is what she wrote:

"If you lived in the year 1870, which is over a hundred years ago, you could not talk on the phone. You could not ride in a car, a plane, or watch TV. These things had not been made yet. People are making things better all the time. Someday when we talk on the phone, we might be able to see the person, too. What else will be made for the people of tomorrow?"

UNIT 8

1. The best title is—

    (A) TV
    (B) Making New Things
    (C) How to Fly a Plane
    (D) Talking on the Phone

2. The story says that in 1870, you could not—

    (A) build a house   (B) ride in a train
    (C) ride in a car   (D) ride in a wagon

3. To find out things to write for her report, Maria—

    (A) went to the library   (B) asked her mom
    (C) went to the store   (D) asked her teacher

4. You can tell that people who think of new things to make are—

    (A) afraid   (B) silly
    (C) smart   (D) sad

5. In the picture, Maria is—

    (A) drawing   (B) eating
    (C) talking   (D) thinking

UNIT 9

Every year there is a special walk for the hungry. People try to walk twenty miles. They find other people who will pay them money for each mile they walk. Then the walkers give this money to help hungry people everywhere.

Last year, Bill joined the walk for the hungry. Bill can't see. Bill's friends helped him. They walked hand in hand. They walked from the city along the river to another town and back again. Bill heard people talking, singing, and laughing as they walked. He felt glad to be part of this walk. The walk took Bill six hours to finish. He was tired but happy.

UNIT 9

1. The best title is—

    (A) Bill Cannot Hear
    (B) Bill Walks for the Hungry
    (C) Hungry People
    (D) A Race

2. In the walk for the hungry, people try to walk—

    (A) 5 miles   (B) 10 miles
    (C) 20 miles   (D) 15 miles

3. In this story, Bill—

    (A) is tall   (B) is smart
    (C) can't hear   (D) can't see

4. Bill probably wanted to go on the walk because—

    (A) he wanted to help   (B) it was on his way home
    (C) it seemed easy   (D) he had sore feet

5. In the picture, the people are walking near a—

    (A) bridge   (B) lawn
    (C) street with cars (D) bus

UNIT 10

"I don't like my new dog. He won't do what I tell him," said Cora. Her new puppy, Ruff, wouldn't even come when she called him. Then Cora's mother found out that Ruff couldn't hear. That was why he didn't do what Cora told him.

So Cora began teaching Ruff to do things by looking at her hands. She taught him to come if she waved her hand, and to sit if she touched the floor.

Cora is glad that she can "talk" to her puppy and he can understand her.

UNIT 10

1. The best title is—

    (A) Teaching Ruff to Eat
    (B) Cora and Her Puppy
    (C) Finding a Lost Cat
    (D) A Bad Dog

2. Cora's dog, Ruff, cannot—

    (A) see   (B) walk
    (C) eat   (D) hear

3. When Cora touches the floor, her dog—

    (A) runs away   (B) begins to bark
    (C) sits   (D) sleeps

4. Ruff knows what Cora wants by using his—

    (A) eyes   (B) nose
    (C) tail   (D) teeth

5. In the picture, the dog is—

    (A) sitting   (B) standing
    (C) sleeping   (D) barking

27

UNIT 11

The children at Lake School are careful when they walk up to their school. They don't want to step on a duck!

Two years ago, a mother duck made her nest in the school's playground. Soon she had six baby ducks. The children and the teachers think that the ducks are cute. Many times the ducks leave the playground and walk around to the front of the school. Everyone is careful not to step on them.

The ducks like the children, and the children like the ducks. They have become the school's pets.

UNIT 11

1. The best title is—

    (A) A Duck Gets Lost
    (B) Fun in the Playground
    (C) Ducks That Are a School's Pets
    (D) A Nice Teacher

2. The mother duck had—

    (A) ten baby ducks
    (B) three baby ducks
    (C) five baby ducks
    (D) six baby ducks

3. The children think the ducks are—

    (A) ugly
    (B) cute
    (C) lazy
    (D) dirty

4. You can tell that the ducks—

    (A) are sick
    (B) are afraid
    (C) like living at the school
    (D) have been hurt many times

5. In the picture, there are—

    (A) ten ducks
    (B) three ducks
    (C) four ducks
    (D) five ducks

UNIT 12

Chang rode down the side of the city street on his bike. In the basket were two bags of food. The food was for the Chen family. Mrs. Chen was sick today, and she could not shop for the food she needed. She had called Chang's mother. Chang said he would get the food for Mrs. Chen.

Chang brought the food to Mrs. Chen. She was in bed. Chang said, "I hope you feel better soon. Do you want me to put the food in its right place?"

Mrs. Chen smiled, "Yes, thank you. You are very kind." She paid Chang for the food. She felt lucky to have such a good neighbor.

UNIT 12

1. The best title is—

    (A) Riding a Bike

    (B) Mrs. Chen

    (C) The Food Store

    (D) Chang Helps Out

2. Mrs. Chen could not go to the food store because—

    (A) it was too far to walk   (B) she was sick

    (C) she didn't have money   (D) it was closed

3. Mrs. Chen felt that Chang was—

    (A) shy   (B) strong

    (C) hungry   (D) kind

4. You can tell that Chang is a—

    (A) helping person   (B) mean person

    (C) funny person   (D) quiet person

5. The picture shows that Chang got to the store by—

    (A) walking   (B) driving a car

    (C) riding a bike   (D) riding a bus

The Second L A P
Language Activity Pages

A. Exercising Your Skill

Look at the pictures in Units 7, 8, 9, and 12. Think about the people. Where are they? On your paper, name the place where the people in each picture are. Then write one thing that tells about where the people are. With your class, talk about the pictures in Units 7, 8, 9, and 12. Have you been to such places? If you have, talk about what you did there and why you went there.

B. Expanding Your Skill

Look at the words in the word box. They tell about people and animals. You met them in the pictures and stories in Units 7 through 12. Now read the names of the people and animals below the box. On your own paper, write the names of these people and animals. Then write the words from the word box that tell about each person or animal.

can ride a bike	cannot hear
writes a story for school	are school pets
likes to ride buses	cannot see

1. Sam Brooks ⎯⎯⎯⎯⎯⎯⎯⎯
2. Maria ⎯⎯⎯⎯⎯⎯⎯⎯⎯⎯
3. Bill ⎯⎯⎯⎯⎯⎯⎯⎯⎯⎯⎯
4. Ruff, a new puppy ⎯⎯⎯⎯
5. Ducks ⎯⎯⎯⎯⎯⎯⎯⎯⎯⎯
6. Chang ⎯⎯⎯⎯⎯⎯⎯⎯⎯

The Second L A P
Language Activity Pages

C. Exploring Language

Look at the picture in Unit 7. Sam is talking to a man on the bus. Pretend that Sam is telling the man about a place he has visited. Write a story about what Sam told the man. First, answer the questions below on your own paper. Then write your story.

Who? __Sam_____
Went where? _____
When? _____
What did he see? _____
What did he do? _____
How did he feel? _____
Did he like his visit? Why or why not? _____
_____

D. Expressing Yourself

Do one of these things.

1. Fold drawing paper into four boxes. Now look at the picture in Unit 11. Pretend that the ducks decide to find a new home. Draw four pictures, one in each box. In the first picture, show the ducks at the school playground. In the last picture, show the ducks at their new home. In the other pictures, show where the ducks went before they found a new home. Write a sentence about each picture.

2. Look at the picture of Chang in Unit 12. On your own paper, draw a picture to show what happens next. Write a sentence about your picture.

UNIT 13

Some people felt that the city playground was falling apart. They wanted to make it into a nice, safe place for children to play.

One mother put this note in the newspaper. "Wanted: People to fix a city playground. We need people to paint and build, to watch the children, and to make food for the workers. Call 555–8723 if you can help."

On the work day, many people came to the playground. Some painted the swings. Others built a sandbox, tables, and benches. People planted bushes and flowers. When it was all done, everyone was proud of the new playground.

UNIT 13

1. The best title is—

    (A) In the City
    (B) A New Playground
    (C) Building a House
    (D) A Picnic

2. People wanted to fix the playground because it—

    (A) didn't have grass   (B) was too small
    (C) was falling apart   (D) was too big

3. People were needed to—

    (A) run in a race   (B) paint and build
    (C) come to a car wash   (D) give money

4. You can tell that the people—

    (A) did not like the new playground
    (B) felt the new playground was too small
    (C) thought the new playground cost too much
    (D) liked the new playground

5. In the picture, you can see people—

    (A) swimming   (B) sitting
    (C) building   (D) crying

UNIT 14

All the children at school love Mr. Rider. He has worked at the school for a long time. Mr. Rider cleans the floors and keeps everything neat. He is very nice to the children, too. He helps them with their schoolwork and often finds things they have lost in school.

One day the children thought, "Let's do something nice for Mr. Rider." They bought him a beautiful tie and a pair of socks. The next morning when Mr. Rider came to work, everyone shouted, "Surprise!" Mr. Rider said it was the best surprise he ever had.

UNIT 14

1. The best title is—

    (A) Finding Lost Things

    (B) Riding on the School Bus

    (C) Children Do Their Schoolwork

    (D) A Surprise for Mr. Rider

2. The story says that Mr. Rider—

    (A) teaches reading	(B) never talks

    (C) cleans the floors	(D) likes to dance

3. The children gave Mr. Rider a—

    (A) kitten	(B) clock

    (C) coat and hat	(D) tie and socks

4. The children made Mr. Rider—

    (A) happy	(B) afraid

    (C) lazy	(D) safe

5. In the picture, the children are—

    (A) painting a picture	(B) smiling

    (C) sitting	(D) playing a game

UNIT 15

Every Monday, when Marge gets out of work, she goes to a special place. There she reads books out loud for people who cannot see.

Marge loves to read. She knows that blind people can read special books with their fingers. But blind people like to share stories by listening to them too. So Marge shares the stories by making recordings of them.

Marge makes a recording for the blind once a week. She reads the story or stories that she likes best. She hopes that those who listen to them will like them as much.

UNIT 15

1. The best title is—

   (A) A Woman Who Writes Stories

   (B) Finding a Lost Book

   (C) Marge Reads for the Blind

   (D) A Trip to the Library

2. The story says that Marge loves to—

   (A) sleep   (B) eat

   (C) read   (D) skate

3. Marge reads books for blind people every—

   (A) Monday   (B) Sunday

   (C) night   (D) day

4. You can tell that Marge—

   (A) cannot talk   (B) cannot hear

   (C) likes flowers (D) can see

5. In the picture, there are—

   (A) two people   (B) three people

   (C) seven people (D) trees

UNIT 16

Most people have dogs or cats as pets. Chris has a different kind of pet. She has a chicken.

Chris went to visit her grandmother. Next door was a chicken farm. One chicken was smaller than the others. The larger chickens always picked on the little chicken. Chris fell in love with it, so the owner of the farm gave it to her.

Chris keeps her pet chicken in her family's garage. She says that her pet is one chicken that will never be given away. She loves it too much.

UNIT 16

1. The best title is—

    (A) A Chicken Farm

    (B) A Pet Chicken

    (C) Cleaning the Garage

    (D) A Long Trip

2. Chris went to visit her—

    (A) uncle   (B) sister

    (C) grandmother   (D) neighbor

3. Chris keeps her pet chicken in—

    (A) the kitchen   (B) the garage

    (C) a bedroom   (D) a barn

4. You can tell that the owner of the farm was—

    (A) Chris' father (B) very young

    (C) a bad farmer   (D) a nice person

5. In the picture, one chicken is—

    (A) swimming   (B) small

    (C) asleep   (D) flying

UNIT 17

Juan watched the older boys play basketball every day. How he wished he would grow taller! He was still too short. Try as hard as he could, he just couldn't throw the ball into the net.

The big boys played ball in an empty lot on a city street. It had once been filled with garbage. The boys had cleaned it up. They had saved their money to buy a ball, pole, and net. Now they came every day to practice.

One day the big boys had a surprise for Juan. They had found a used pole and net just the right size for him. Now Juan is there every day, not watching but playing.

UNIT 17

1. The best title is—

    (A) Playing Baseball
    (B) Saving Money
    (C) An Empty Lot
    (D) A Surprise for Juan

2. Juan wished that he—

    (A) had more money
    (B) would grow taller
    (C) had a dog
    (D) could run fast

3. The surprise for Juan was a—

    (A) pole and net just his size
    (B) ticket to a game
    (C) new baseball cap
    (D) new ball

4. The boys cleaned up the lot so they could—

    (A) plant a garden
    (B) make money
    (C) play baseball
    (D) play basketball

5. In this picture, you can see—

    (A) a bus
    (B) a dog
    (C) a fence
    (D) flowers

UNIT 18

Mrs. Ball got a little puppy for a pet. She named it Tiger. One day, Tiger came into the house with Mrs. Ball's newspaper in his mouth. He put it on her chair. Mrs. Ball thought it was a cute trick. She gave Tiger a special treat.

The next day, Mrs. Ball went to sit down. There were ten newspapers on her chair! Where had they come from? Then she saw Tiger wagging his tail. Tiger had gone to all the houses on their block. He had taken the newspapers from the porches and brought them home. He wanted some more treats!

UNIT 18

1. The best title is—

    (A) Mrs. Ball Reads the Newspaper
    (B) Tiger Brings Newspapers Home
    (C) Mrs. Ball Finds a Lost Dog
    (D) A Dog That Wags Its Tail

2. Tiger put the newspapers on a—

    (A) chair   (B) table
    (C) box   (D) bed

3. Tiger got the ten newspapers from—

    (A) a store   (B) a friend
    (C) garages   (D) porches

4. You can tell that Tiger likes—

    (A) to read   (B) to sleep
    (C) treats   (D) eggs

5. In the picture, you can see—

    (A) a hat   (B) a chair
    (C) two dogs   (D) red shoes

UNIT 19

A letter came for Wanda. It asked her to come to a party. The person who dressed in the most different way would win a prize.

Many young people came to the party. One boy was dressed as a tree. A girl looked like a rabbit. All the people looked good. Then they picked the person who looked the most unusual. Wanda won!

Wanda looked like a bunch of grapes. She had a hat with a stem, and balloons pinned to her clothes. The balloons were hanging all around her. Wanda was the most real-looking bunch of grapes the other people had ever seen!

UNIT 19

1. The best title is—

    (A) Wanda Wins a Prize
    (B) A Funny Clown
    (C) Wanda Loses a Letter
    (D) Picking Up Leaves

2. The story says that a boy dressed as—

    (A) a fish   (B) a rabbit
    (C) a tree   (D) an elephant

3. Wanda looked like a—

    (A) rabbit   (B) baby
    (C) grandmother   (D) bunch of grapes

4. Wanda looked like something that—

    (A) flies   (B) quacks
    (C) grows   (D) swims

5. In the picture, one person is dressed like a—

    (A) house   (B) rabbit
    (C) box   (D) book

The Third L A P
Language Activity Pages

A. Exercising Your Skill

Look at the word map below. All the words in the boxes are alike in some way. One of the words in the circle tells how they are alike. Can you tell how? Write that word from the circle on your paper.

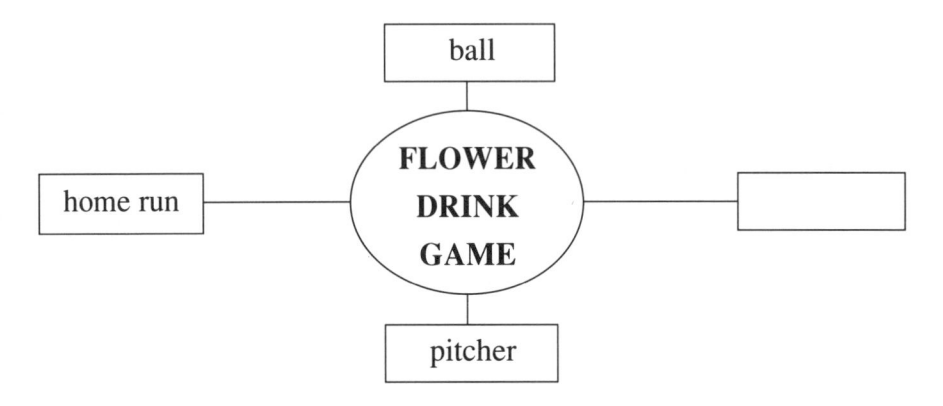

```
                    ┌──────┐
                    │ ball │
                    └──────┘
                       │
              ╭────────────────╮
┌──────────┐  │    FLOWER      │  ┌──────────┐
│ home run │──│    DRINK       │──│          │
└──────────┘  │    GAME        │  └──────────┘
              ╰────────────────╯
                       │
                  ┌─────────┐
                  │ pitcher │
                  └─────────┘
```

Tell a classmate the word you wrote. Did your classmate write the same word? Together think of four other words to go with the word in the circle. Make a new word map on your paper. Write the four words you thought of in the boxes.

B. Expanding Your Skill

Read the words in the word box. Then read each list of words. The words in the box tell where you can find the things in each list. On your paper, write 1, 2, and 3 and the place that fits each list.

playground	school	farm

1. At a _____
   barn
   animals

2. At a _____
   sandbox
   swings

3. At a _____
   desks
   books

48

The Third L A P
Language Activity Pages

C. Exploring Language

Below is a story that starts like the story in Unit 16. But this story has a different ending. On your own paper, write a good title for the story.

(Title)

One chicken was smaller than all the others. The larger chickens always picked on the little chicken. The little chicken felt that no one liked it. It wanted to run away from the farm. But it was too afraid of the big world outside the pen. So the little chicken stayed.

On your paper, write three or four more sentences to go with this story. Tell about the day when the little chicken was brave enough to leave. Tell what happened. When you finish, write a new title.

D. Expressing Yourself

Do one of these things.

1. Write a short story on your own paper. Pick one of the ideas below.

    - A Game I Like to Play
    - My Favorite Animal
    - A Big Surprise
    - The Party

    When you write your story, have the first sentence tell what the story will be about.

2. Play the game "Ten Questions." Think of a person, animal, place, or thing. Have a classmate ask you questions that you can answer "yes" or "no." See how many questions it takes for your classmate to guess what you thought about. Don't forget to stop at "ten"!

UNIT 20

All the people on his street call Mr. Parks the fix-it man. Whenever anything needs fixing, he comes with his tools and a big smile. Mr. Parks no longer works at a job all day. He has time to do what he likes best—fixing things.

Last week, he fixed a drip in Mrs. Lane's sink. He fixed the steps on Mr. Barker's back porch. He helped the children on the street fix up the old tree house so it looked new.

One day Mr. Parks' wife said, "Our window needs to be fixed!" Mr. Parks had been so busy helping others, he had forgotten to fix his own window. "I'll fix it right away," said Mr. Parks.

UNIT 20

1. The best title is—

    (A) The Fix-it Man
    (B) A Broken Window
    (C) Fixing Teeth
    (D) A Tree House

2. What Mr. Parks likes to do best is—

    (A) eat
    (B) read books
    (C) fix things
    (D) take trips

3. Mr. Parks fixed Mrs. Lane's—

    (A) chair
    (B) sink
    (C) door
    (D) steps

4. You can tell that Mr. Parks is—

    (A) strange
    (B) lazy
    (C) sad
    (D) kind

5. In the picture, Mr. Parks is holding a—

    (A) glass
    (B) saw
    (C) hammer
    (D) basket

UNIT 21

Tina and her family moved into a new house. The first night, after Tina had gone to bed, she heard a noise. She got up and looked around, but no one was there. The next night she heard the noise again. It was coming from her bedroom wall. Tina ran and told her parents.

The following day, Tina's father made a hole in the wall. He found a little mouse. Her father took it to the woods and let it go.

UNIT 21

1. The best title is—

    (A) Tina Hears a Mouse

    (B) Tina and Her Pet Dog

    (C) Sleeping in the Kitchen

    (D) Making New Friends

2. The mouse was in Tina's—

    (A) coat   (B) hat

    (C) bedroom wall   (D) big trunk

3. Tina's father took the mouse to the—

    (A) zoo   (B) circus

    (C) lake   (D) woods

4. The noise Tina heard was—

    (A) made by the rain   (B) made by the mouse

    (C) coming from the kitchen   (D) very loud

5. In the picture, the girl is—

    (A) sleeping   (B) reading

    (C) in bed   (D) outside

UNIT 22

A family of squirrels lives in a woods. Every morning the squirrels cross a road to play and to get food. Later in the day, they cross the road again to go back to the woods.

One day, the squirrels were crossing the road. Mr. Alan was driving down the road. He saw the squirrels crossing the road. He said, "I'm afraid that someone will hit those squirrels." So Mr. Alan made a big sign. It said "Watch for Squirrels." He put it by the road, where drivers can see it. He hopes that the sign will keep the squirrels safe from cars.

UNIT 22

1. The best title is—

    (A) A Lost Pet

    (B) A Busy Road

    (C) Mr. Alan Helps the Squirrels

    (D) Why Squirrels Like to Eat

2. The squirrels crossed a—

    (A) road   (B) pond

    (C) river   (D) stream

3. The story says that Mr. Alan made a—

    (A) fence   (B) sign

    (C) toy   (D) basket

4. You can tell that the squirrels sleep—

    (A) on a pond   (B) on the road

    (C) in the woods   (D) in a house

5. In the picture, the squirrels are—

    (A) in a car   (B) crossing a road

    (C) swimming   (D) flying

UNIT 23

Most people like to eat cookies. Nora Jacobson likes to save cookie jars. She has over 180 of them.

Years ago, most homes had a cookie jar. When someone made cookies, they were put into the jar. Nora has cookie jars that look like clowns, cats, houses, and rabbits. She even has a jar that looks like a sheep. When the cover is taken off, it says, "Baa."

Nora is still saving cookie jars. Someday she hopes to have over two hundred—and every one will be different from the rest.

UNIT 23

1. The best title is—

    (A) Why People Like to Eat Cookies

    (B) A Jar That Looks like a House

    (C) Nora and Her Cookie Jars

    (D) A Wonderful Party

2. One of Nora's jars says—

    (A) meow (B) baa

    (C) arf (D) tweet

3. Nora has cookie jars that look like—

    (A) cars (B) clowns

    (C) tables (D) eggs

4. Some of Nora's jars look like—

    (A) animals (B) trees

    (C) airplanes (D) money

5. In the picture, the woman is—

    (A) driving a car (B) in a store

    (C) by a lake (D) holding a jar

UNIT 24

One day the circus came to the city on a special train. Many people came to watch the circus unload. They came to see the parade. The people and animals in the circus came down one of the city streets. They were going to the place where the circus tent would be set up. The band played. The elephants walked holding tails and trunks. The cages of the tigers and bears rolled by on trucks. Clowns handed out balloons to children.

The people in the tall buildings stopped their work when they heard the music. They watched from their windows and cheered.

UNIT 24

1. The best title is—

    (A) The Circus Train
    (B) Clowns
    (C) A Circus Parade
    (D) A Band Plays Music

2. The clowns gave the children—

    (A) apples   (B) balloons
    (C) peanuts   (D) hats

3. In the parade, the elephants—

    (A) rode in trucks   (B) roared
    (C) walked   (D) ran

4. The people in the tall buildings stopped work because—

    (A) it was time for lunch   (B) the circus parade was coming
    (C) it was night   (D) they were tired

5. In the picture, you do *not* see—

    (A) cars   (B) balloons
    (C) clowns   (D) a band

UNIT 25

Lois lives on a farm. Her father gave her a cow to take care of. Lois liked her cow, but it gave only two pails of milk every day. "I wish my cow would give more milk," said Lois.

Then Lois thought, "Maybe if I'm very nice to my cow, it will give more milk." Lois began talking to the cow. She even sang songs to it.

Soon, the cow was giving four pails of milk every day. Lois said, "I'm nice to my cow, and now it's being nice to me."

UNIT 25

1. The best title is—

    (A) Growing Corn on a Farm

    (B) Why a Cow Gave More Milk

    (C) A Cow Runs Away

    (D) A Girl Who Liked to Ride Horses

2. To be nice to her cow, Lois—

    (A) stayed away   (B) walked it

    (C) sang songs   (D) shouted at it

3. Lois got her cow from her—

    (A) mother   (B) father

    (C) uncle   (D) sister

4. When her cow gave four pails of milk a day, Lois felt—

    (A) proud   (B) unhappy

    (C) afraid   (D) tired

5. In the picture, there is—

    (A) a car   (B) a TV

    (C) an animal   (D) a lake

The Last L A P
Language Activity Pages

A. Exercising Your Skill

In Unit 23 Nora Jacobson saves cookie jars. On your own paper, make a list of things that people can save. Put a ✓ next to something you save. Put a + next to something that a person you know saves. After you write your list, share it with the class. Talk about why you think people save things.

Things People Save
_____
_____
_____
_____

B. Expanding Your Skill

The words in the box name things that people save. Read each sentence. From the clues, decide what each person might save. On your paper, write the number of the sentence, the person's name, and what he or she might save.

sea shells	pictures	hats	baseball cards
tools	post cards	books	stuffed animals

1. Pam likes small, soft things.
2. Sam's head is always cold.
3. Lou likes sports.
4. Kim visits the ocean each summer.
5. Rosa can fix anything that breaks.
6. Hal loves to read.
7. Mary loves to visit different places.

The Last L A P
Language Activity Pages

C. Exploring Language

Pretend you save stuffed animals. What might happen if you came home from school one day and your stuffed animals could talk and move about? Write a short story. Before you begin to write, get some ideas for your story. Maybe these questions will help you.

- Do all the animals like each other?
- Do they like the room where you keep them?
- Would they like to have a parade or a party?
    Which would they pick to have?
- Would they ask you to join them?
- Would everyone have fun? Why?

D. Expressing Yourself

Do one of these things.

1. If you could save anything you wanted to, what would it be? Why? Draw a picture of what you want to save. Write a sentence to tell what you would save and why.

2. Pick a story in this book. With your classmates, act out the story. Have one person tell the story. Have enough people to take the parts of each person or animal in the story. Practice what you will do and say. Then act out the story for your class.

3. Think of something different to do with one of these things: a hat, a towel, a pan. You may do something funny, or you may use the thing in a silly way. On your own paper, write a sentence that tells how you would use the thing you picked.